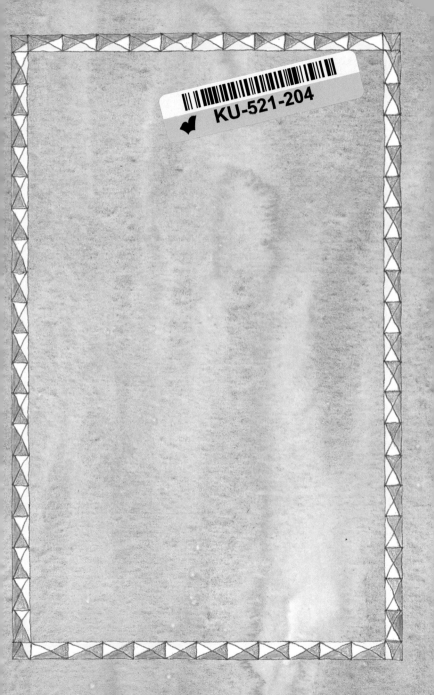

NOTE TO PARENTS

This familiar Bible story has been retold in a sensitive and simple way so that young children can read and understand it for themselves. But the special message of the story remains unchanged. It is the message of God's love and care for us all.

The Boy Jesus

retold by Marjorie Newman
illustrated by Edgar Hodges

Copyright © 1990 by World International Publishing Limited.
All rights reserved.
Published in Great Britain by World International Publishing Limited,
An Egmont Company, Egmont House,
P.O. Box 111, Great Ducie Street,
Manchester M60 3BL.
Printed in DDR.
ISBN 0 7235 4464 6

A CIP catalogue record for this book is available from the British Library.

Jesus lived in a little white house in Nazareth. He lived with Joseph and Mary.

The house had just one room! Every night Jesus, Joseph and Mary slept on mat-beds. And every morning they would hear the cock crow — *cock a doodle do*! Time to get up!

When breakfast was over, Jesus loved to help Mary. First they would shake the dust from the mat-beds. Then Jesus would roll them up and stand them by the wall.

Next, the room would have to be swept.

One day, Mary cried, "I've lost one of my coins!" Jesus helped her search *everywhere.* At last He found it, behind a water jar. Mary and Jesus were very glad!

Now they had to get water from the village well.
Along the dusty street they went. Mary carried the
large water-jar. Jesus carried a small one.

It was fun at the well! There were other mothers
to talk to. There were children to play with. And
Jesus loved to watch Mary filling the water-jars.
Glug, glug, glug!

Sometimes, Mary and Jesus went shopping in the market place. That was fun, too! Jesus helped to carry the things they bought.

Back home again, it was time for Mary to bake the bread. Sometimes Jesus would fetch sticks for Mary to put on the fire.

Or He might go into the carpenter's shop, to help Joseph. Tap, tap, tap, went their hammers. *Zzzzzzzz, zzzzzzzz, zzzzzzzz,* went their saws!

By supper time all the work was done. Then Jesus, Joseph and Mary might climb on to the flat roof of their house. In the starlight Joseph would tell stories to Jesus. And he would teach Him verses of Scripture.

One night Mary suddenly whispered, "Look!" A fox and her cubs were trotting along the road!

"I love them!" said Jesus. "I love all the animals! And the birds!"

"God our Father loves them, too," said Joseph.

On the Sabbath day, the family went to the synagogue church. Jesus sat with Joseph. Mary sat with the other women. Jesus listened hard. He tried to understand all the words.

As soon as Jesus was six years old, He went to the synagogue school. He learned many verses off by heart. And He learned to read, and write, and do sums. At first He wrote with His finger in the sand! And He read from a scroll.

As He grew older, He learned many things. And He had many questions to ask. Sometimes the questions seemed too hard for His teacher . . .

Every springtime many people journeyed to Jerusalem for a special feast. When Jesus was twelve years old, Joseph and Mary took *Him*! It was the custom. Some of His friends were going, as well.

It was a three day journey. At last they reached Jerusalem. Jesus couldn't *wait* to visit the Temple. He knew He would find some very clever teachers there. He wanted to listen to them, and ask questions.

The people from Nazareth stayed in Jerusalem
for a whole week. Every day Jesus went to the
Temple. The teachers were surprised at how much
He knew about God. And they had never known a
boy who asked such questions!

At last it was time to go home. Mary and Joseph set out with the others. They thought Jesus was with His friends. But He was missing! What could have happened to Him?

Jesus must still be in Jerusalem. Fearfully, Mary and Joseph hurried back to the city. They searched everywhere.

At last they reached the Temple. Surely Jesus wouldn't be here! He'd spent seven days here already!

Joseph and Mary stood still. For there, still talking with the teachers, was Jesus.

"Jesus!" cried Mary. "We thought you were lost!"

Jesus looked surprised. "Didn't you *know* I would be in my Heavenly Father's house?" He said.

"It's time to leave," said Joseph. "Come." At once Jesus obeyed Joseph. Then Mary, Joseph and Jesus went back to Nazareth. And there Jesus grew up.

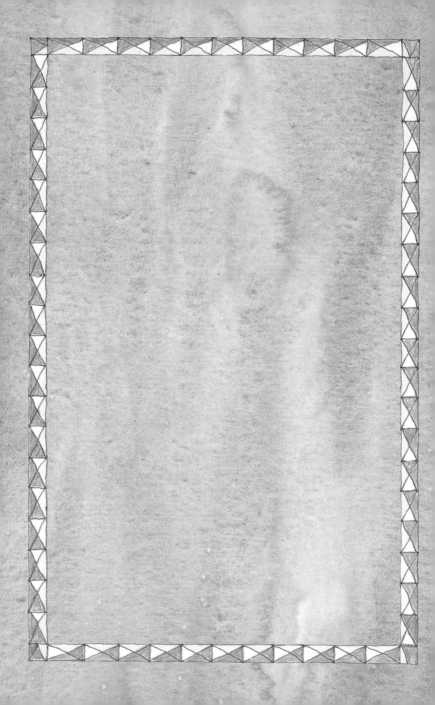